SPRING IS FUN!

by Walt K. Moon

BUMBA BOOKS™

LERNER PUBLICATIONS ◆ MINNEAPOLIS

Note to Educators:

Throughout this book, you'll find critical thinking questions. These can be used to engage young readers in thinking critically about the topic and in using the text and photos to do so.

Lerner Publications Company
A division of Lerner Publishing Group, Inc.
241 First Avenue North
Minneapolis, MN 55401 USA

For reading levels and more information, look up this title at www.lernerbooks.com.

Library of Congress Cataloging-in-Publication Data

The Cataloging-in-Publication Data for *Spring Is Fun!* is on file at the Library of Congress.
ISBN 978-1-5124-1411-0 (lib. bdg.)
ISBN 978-1-5124-1531-5 (pbk.)
ISBN 978-1-5124-1532-2 (EB pdf)

Manufactured in the United States of America
1 — VP — 7/15/16

LERNER
SOURCE™

Expand learning beyond the printed book. Download free, complementary educational resources for this book from our website, www.lerneresource.com.

Table of Contents

Spring Season

Each year has

four seasons.

Spring is one season.

Temperatures warm up

in spring.

Spring comes after the cold winter.

Snow melts.

Its water fills rivers and streams.

The ground becomes wet.

What makes snow melt in spring?

Rain falls too.

Grass and plants begin

to grow.

Flowers bloom in spring.

They have bright colors.

Why do you think flowers have bright colors?

Farmers plant their crops.

They put seeds in the dirt.

The plants take months to grow.

Animals have babies in spring.

Baby birds chirp.

Why do you think baby birds chirp?

Some animals migrate.

A goose moves to a warmer place

in winter.

It comes back in spring.

It is warm again.

Easter eggs

Spring has many

fun holidays.

People celebrate

Passover and Easter.

May Day is on May 1.

People go outside more in spring.

Some play baseball.

Others hike.

What do you do in spring?

20

Seasons Cycle

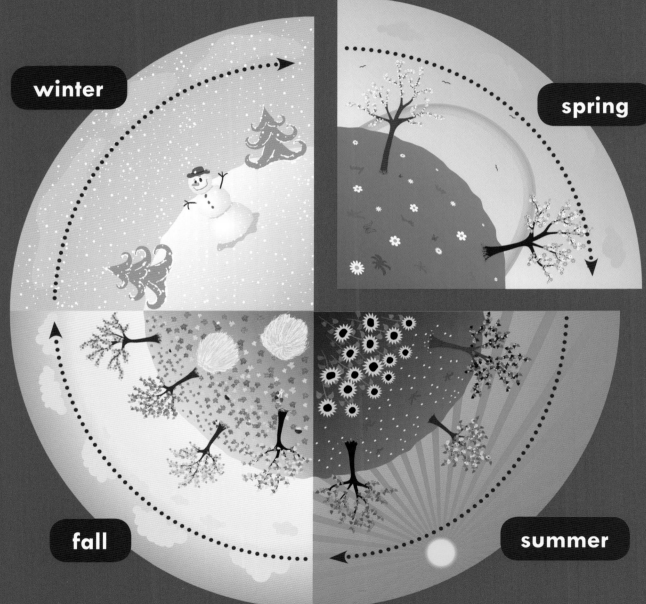

winter

spring

fall

summer

Picture Glossary

bloom

to produce flowers

chirp

to make a sound

crops

plants grown for food or goods

migrate

to move to another area at a certain time of year

Index

Read More

Anderson, Sheila. *Are You Ready for Spring?* Minneapolis: Lerner Publications, 2010.

Gleisner, Jenna Lee. *What Blossoms in Spring?* Ann Arbor, MI: Cherry Lake Publishing, 2015.

Herrington, Lisa M. *How Do You Know It's Spring?* New York: Children's Press, 2014.

Photo Credits